The Powerful Little No Rapture Book

What the Bible Says About a Rapture

By Dr Peter Wyns

Copyright © 2019 by Dr. Peter D. Wyns

Christians for Messiah Publishing
PO Box 36324
Rock Hill, SC 29732
www.peterwyns.com
email: wynsusa@comporium.net

All Scriptures used, unless otherwise indicated, are taken from the New International Version. Scriptures taken from the Holy Bible, New International Version ® Copyright © 1973, 1978, 1984 by International Bible Society. Any underlining words within passages indicate the emphasis of this author.

All rights reserved. No part of this publication may be reproduced without written permission of Christians for Messiah Publishing

Cover Design by: Judy Wilson and Elizabeth Enns
Editing by: Jesse Enns and Rachel Enns

First Christians for Messiah Publishing edition published 2019.
Manufactured in the United States of America.

ISBN: 978-0-9915421-5-4

About the Author

Dr. Peter Wyns comes from a family of preachers and Bible teachers. He is the grandson of Derek Prince. Through 50 years of ministry Dr. Wyns has planted 7 churches, and ministered in over 40 nations. He is the president of Christians for Messiah Ministries and Head Pastor at Antioch International Church. He speaks at conferences, church meetings, Bible schools and leadership training seminars across the USA and abroad. He ministers on a wide variety of Bible themes.

Other books written by Dr. Wyns include:

Unexpected Fire: The Book of Revelation
Poetic Fire: Understanding the Book of Revelation (poetry)
America in the Last Days: The Jonah Nation
Blessings or Curses for the Next Generation
Prayer that Hits the Target
Israel's Coming Revival
Great Reward for Kids – volumes 1-3
Chronicles of Righteousness – volumes 1-3
Fighting Death and other Desperate Battles

To order these or any other materials, please visit www.peterwyns.com

Table of Contents

Part One: Biblical Proof - No Rapture

Chapter One ....…..…The No Rapture Challenge

Chapter Two ……....…………..…The Lord Will Descend

Chapter Three …………..……….The Gathering of the Saints

Chapter Four ………………………………..... Two In the Field

Chapter Five ……………….………… No Wrath for Saints

Part Two: Additional No Rapture Verses

Chapter Six …………………..…..….. Jesus Stays in Heaven

Chapter Seven …………………….… Saints Ready for War

Chapter Eight …………….. The Days of the Last Trumpet

Chapter Nine ………………..…. Friend of the Bride Groom

Chapter Ten ……………….………...……….. The Ten Virgins

Chapter Eleven ………….. Coming Back in the Same Way

Chapter Twelve ………… Rapture Teaching is Dangerous

Part One

Biblical Proof - No Rapture

Chapter One

The No Rapture Challenge

A Popular Doctrine

The doctrine of the rapture is so widespread and popular among evangelicals that many receive it as unquestionable Gospel. We have heard many sermons and read so many scriptures about the rapture that we think it must be true. To even imagine that there is no rapture may seem ridiculous to those who have been taught it with such fervor. Some may even think that the people who do not believe in the rapture are uneducated, unlearned and non-spiritual. Others, who are extremists, may even think that the no-rapture people are probably not saved, or they don't have the Holy Spirit. As you will discover, this is definitely not true.

Rapture's Starting Point

In this book I will show you that Jesus and the disciples taught about the resurrection, but they did not teach about a rapture. Nor did the early apostles, the apostolic fathers, or the church fathers. The early monks did not speak of a pre-trib-rapture, nor did reformers such as Martin Luther or John Calvin. The great revivalists like John Wesley, George Whitfield, Charles Finney, Charles Spurgeon, RA Torrey, DL Moody, and Jonathan Edwards never preached about a pre-trib-rapture because they did not believe in it. In fact, the pre-trib-rapture teaching is brand new.

Rapture theology, in general, only began in the 18th century. It started with Puritans under the leadership of Cotton Mather. Then in the 1830's, John Darby made the pre-trib-rapture idea popular within the Plymouth Brethren church. The pre-trib-rapture doctrine was not taught before 1830. After that, it became more acceptable within the United States' evangelical church because of the footnotes that were included in the Scofield Reference Bible. That Bible was widely circulated in the early part of the 20th century. Since then, the rapture has become a mainstay of evangelical thought in America and in parts of the world where the evangelical church of America has planted congregations. The rest of the Christian church around the world, by and large, does not embrace this teaching.

The teaching began because, in John Darby's day, some Christians believed, the false doctrine, that the Church itself, would bring about the millennial reign of God's kingdom without Christ's second coming. Other Christians believed that there would never be a millennium of God's kingdom on earth. Mr. Darby stepped up to correct these false doctrines and it was then that he caught hold of this idea of a pre-tribulation rapture. It had not been taught before then.

As mentioned earlier, this new idea was embraced by Dr. C. I. Scofield and put in the footnotes of his new reference Bible. Without proper Bible study or Biblical proofs, leaders of the evangelical church took the Scofield footnotes as gospel and from there the teaching became popular. It is time we did a proper Bible study on the subject. I do not want you to think that I am the first teacher to broach the subject and find it to be in error. If you search, you will discover a large number of theologians and Bible students who agree that the Bible never speaks of a pre-trib-rapture.

A Wake Up Call

I encourage you to set your emotions aside. Don't be angry when you see what the Bible really says on the subject of a rapture. After reading this study, some of you will think you have been duped all these years, that you have been tricked or deceived by the Bible teachers you trusted. I am sure they did not mean to deceive you, they simply did not know.

It is not my aim in life to be controversial, nor to put other Bible teachers in a bad light. I do not desire to rub the truth in the face of other teachers. All of us are on a journey for truth. Disciples agree that the Bible is the final court of appeal for sound doctrine. So come with me and I will show you what the Bible says about a rapture. Let us be like the Bereans in Acts 17:11, who received the Word with readiness of mind and searched the Scriptures to see whether these things were true. This is an important matter so let us begin.

The Pre-Trib-Rapture

We must first ask ourselves, what do most Christians mean when they refer to the rapture? For most rapturists, it is about a pre-trib-rapture and that is what we will be studying. The popular pre-tribulation rapture doctrine states that when Jesus Christ returns to earth, He takes His people up to heaven so they may escape the great tribulation.

In more detail, He descends from heaven to the clouds and the dead in Christ will rise. Then, those in Christ who are alive and remain are caught up together with Him in the clouds. Then, rapture theorists add something that is not in the Bible. They teach that suddenly Jesus turns around and takes these disciples back to heaven. They say this because the verse states, " And so they shall ever be with the Lord." 1 Thes. 4:17

The first part of this explanation is true according to the scripture in 1 Thessalonians 4:17. The last part about going back to heaven, however, is not in the book of Thessalonians. In fact, it is not in the Bible at all.

There is a resurrection and a catching up into the clouds, but Jesus does not turn around, and there is no pre-trib-rapture up to heaven. Don't be discouraged and do not be afraid, Christians have an amazing future in the last days.

In our study

1. We will look at the second coming of the Lord and what happens when He returns.

2. We will investigate the scriptures that talk about two people in the field or two in the bed, when one is taken and the other is left.

3. We will discover what the Bible says about the saints not suffering the wrath of God or coming under the judgments of heaven.

4. We will study the chronology of the end-times so that we will have an accurate timeline of the last days.

5. We will discover what the Bible says about the resurrection.

6. We will do our best to investigate every verse that is used to support a rapture theory. We will show you how each one of those verses fails to support that theory. In fact these verses tell us plainly that there is no rapture.

7. We will look at how dangerous a rapture theory can be to the plans and purposes of God and to His Church.

Students of the Scriptures

We do not have to guess at any of these details for all of them are clearly explained in God's word. Be prepared, you may have to unlearn something that you were previously taught. It is not a matter of one person's opinion over another's. We are not talking about different perspectives, as if the Bible is ambiguous on the subject. We can get the truth from God's word. On this subject, we are not left to diversity of scriptural ideas. If we are Bible students, then we are not left with the option of non-biblical interpretations. The Bible is so clear regarding the teaching of the second coming and the resurrection of the saints. It is definitive.

We all know that the issue is not how many people teach a doctrine that makes it correct. At the end of the day, the only thing that matters is what the Bible says. Once we discover what the scriptures say on a subject, we who are disciples are predisposed to follow that truth and not to prop up or hold fast to an incorrect bias.

Whether in the business world or in the Church world, change is difficult for many people. When there is a change of mindset or a new product that comes on the market, there are three groups of people who will embrace it.

1. The first group are pioneers. They are the few who blaze the trail to discover what is true and what is best.

2. Then comes the second group. They are many in number. They walk in the new truth or receive the better product because its benefits become evident.

3. The third group are also seekers of truth but they are cautious so they wait until a product or a teaching has been proven over time before they commit.

What group will you be in; the first, second, or third? (Definitely, if you are a diligent disciple you will be in one of these groups.) A huge shift of doctrine is coming regarding the rapture. Be prepared for a shift in your thinking. I trust this book will help you.

Chapter Two

The Lord Will Descend

A Place to Start

We are at the start of our study so let us begin where most people begin when they defend the rapture doctrine. We will go to the scripture that rapture theorists use to start their argument.

"For the Lord himself will come down from heaven, with a loud command, with the voice of the archangel and with the trumpet call of God, and the dead in Christ will rise first. After that, we who are still alive and are left will be caught up together with them in the clouds to meet the Lord in the air. And so we will be with the Lord forever." 1 Thes. 4:15

Christians agree, the Lord Jesus is coming back again. We love His appearing and we cry, "Lord Jesus Come quickly."

The Spirit and the bride say come! Darkness will cover the earth and gross darkness will cover the people (Isa. 60:2). It will be in a time of trouble that the Lord will come and only the second coming of Christ will solve the problems of the planet. As believers, we have this hope and are unwavering in our resolve. These biblical facts are non-negotiable. Regardless of the timing, all of us say with a unified heart, *"Come Lord Jesus!"*

When and how He comes is therefore extremely vital to our theology, because our thinking will determine our behavior. So let us be careful; we must not add to the scriptures nor take away from them. Jesus comes in the clouds, and the dead are raised. Then, the living, who love Him, are caught up together with them in the clouds to meet the Lord in the air.

The verse, however, does not say we are taken back to heaven. It says that from that point on, we will forever be with the Lord. Therefore, we must ask the question, "Where is Jesus going?" for that is where we will be.

Jesus Descends

There are at least two places in the Bible that tell us where He is going after the gathering in the clouds. In both of these places, the scriptures say that Jesus descends to the earth. He does not go back to heaven. If we will forever be with the Lord, then when he comes to the earth, we will come to the earth with Him.

1. This is first recorded in Zechariah.

We read:

"Then the Lord will go out and fight against those nations, as he fights on a day of battle. <u>On that day his feet will stand on the Mount of Olives, east of Jerusalem</u> … The Lord will be king over the whole earth. On that day there will be one Lord, and his name the only name." Zec. 14:3,4,9

This is clearly the second coming of Christ. It happens during a time of war. Jesus lands on the Mount of Olives. Then, He rescues the planet and begins His millennium rule on the earth. The Bible does not say that Jesus returns to heaven but that

His feet stand on the Mount of Olives in Jerusalem.

2. Another place that the Bible speaks of Christ's descent to the planet is at the end of the book of Revelation.

It says:

"I saw heaven standing open and there before me was a white horse, whose rider is called Faithful and True. With justice he judges and wages war. His eyes are like blazing fire and on his head are many crowns. He has a name written on him that no one knows but he himself. He is dressed in a robe dipped in blood, and his name is the Word of God. The armies of heaven were following him, riding on white horses and dressed in fine linen, white and clean. Coming out of his mouth was a sharp sword with which <u>to strike down the nations</u>. "He will rule them with an iron scepter." He treads the winepress of the fury of the wrath of God Almighty. On his robe and on his thigh he has this name written: King of Kings and Lord of Lords ... Then I saw <u>the beast and the kings of the earth and their armies gathered together</u>

to wage war against the rider on the horse and his army." Rev. 19:11-16, 19

In these two passages, we discover that Jesus descends to the earth. He leaves heaven, comes into the clouds, and resurrects His Church in a twinkling of an eye. Then He descends down to the earth and fights a battle. There is absolutely no mention of Him returning to heaven.

Chronological Revelation

At the end of the Bible, we discover the second coming of Christ. Jesus comes out of heaven and descends to the earth on a white horse. After resurrecting His people, He immediately strikes down the evil people of the nations and fights a battle against the beast and the kings of the earth. Within a few verses, we discover that He defeats His enemies and throws the Antichrist and the False Prophet into the lake of fire. So Jesus destroys the Antichrist at His coming.

This account from Revelation 19 is the second coming and there is no third coming in the Bible. People will continue to have wrong doctrine and misguided ideas if they make things up that are not in the Bible.

Throughout the Old and New Testaments, the Bible speaks of Christ's return. In the gospels, Jesus spoke of His second coming. Where do people find a third coming? It is not in the Bible yet in order to substantiate the rapture, a third coming is invented.

Please note; the second coming happens at the end of the book of Revelation. It takes place in the 19th chapter and there are only 22 chapters in the book. The second coming does not take place before the great tribulation. The great tribulation begins in chapter 6. There is no mention of an Antichrist before those chapters and there is no mention of Christ coming before those chapters either.

The book of Revelation happens in chronological order. This fact is so important. The book begins with John receiving a vision and it ends with judgment, a lake of fire, and saints ruling on the earth with Christ. Revelation progresses through 7 seals, 7 trumpets, and 7 bowls of wrath; one follows the other in order. The book is so chronological and it is inappropriate to mix up the order of events to fit one's perspective. Revelation is so clearly laid out, step by step. One key to understanding Revelation is to keep it in the order it is given. It follows that the 6th seal is not removed before the 2nd seal is removed. The 7th trumpet is not blown before the 1st trumpet is blown. The bowls of wrath are not poured out before the scroll is opened and so on. The book of Revelation is given, line by line in chronological sequence. In order to try to substantiate a rapture, teachers have moved verses out of position and placed them where they do not belong and in so doing, they add things that are not in the text. Revelation 22:18 gives the reader a serious warning. It tells us that the judgments written in the book will come upon any who add or take away from this text. We need to be very careful about how we handle this book.

Chapter Three

The Gathering of the Saints

If There Was a Rapture

There is a definitive scripture that talks about the second coming of the Lord and our being gathered unto Him. If there were a rapture in the Bible, this would be the chapter and verse to describe it. Rather than point to a rapture, however, this chapter tells us that a pre-trib-rapture does not exist.

"Concerning the coming of our Lord Jesus Christ and our being gathered to him ... Don't let anyone deceive you in any way, for <u>that day will not come until the rebellion occurs and the man of lawlessness is revealed</u>, the man doomed to destruction. He will oppose and will exalt himself over everything that is called God or is worshipped, so that he sets himself up in God's temple, proclaiming himself to be God ... the lawless one will be revealed, whom the Lord Jesus will overthrow with the

breath of his mouth <u>and destroy by the splendor of his coming</u>." 2 Thes. 2:1,3,4,8

If there was ever a scripture that pointed to a rapture this would be it. This scripture says, "Now concerning the coming of our Lord Jesus Christ and our being gathered to him."

This scripture speaks of being gathered to Christ but not about a rapture to heaven. It also tells us another important detail. It says that at the second coming, when we are gathered to Christ, that the Antichrist is killed.

Notice, two important details in these verses.

1. The Antichrist must be revealed before the second coming of Christ (2 Thes. 2:3).

2. The Antichrist will be destroyed at the same time the second coming of Christ takes place (2 Thes. 2:8).

If the Antichrist is destroyed at the second coming then how can Christ come at the beginning of the tribulation? If that happened there would be no Antichrist in the great tribulation. Scripture tells us the Antichrist is the major demonic force during the *last* half of the great tribulation. Therefore, Christ's second coming occurs after the great tribulation.

The Antichrist Revealed

The Antichrist is not revealed until after the 7 seals are broken off the scroll, and the 7 trumpets have been blown. There are 22 chapters in Revelation and the beast is revealed in chapter 13, at the halfway point of the book. The beast is revealed at the halfway point of the great tribulation. Notice, the reference in Revelation 13:

"And I saw a beast ... It had ten horns and seven heads." Rev. 13:1

The beast is the Antichrist. According to scripture, Christ cannot come until after the Antichrist is revealed. This means that Christ cannot come at the beginning of the great tribulation. He cannot come before Revelation chapter 13. So there is no pre-trib-second coming and there is no pre-trib-rapture.

The Antichrist Destroyed

The second important detail in 2 Thessalonians 2 is that the beast is destroyed at Christ's second coming, when we are gathered together unto Him.

"the lawless one will be revealed, whom <u>the Lord Jesus will overthrow with the breath of his mouth and destroy by the splendor of his coming</u>." 2 Thes. 2:8

When we read the book of Revelation, we discover that all of this happens in the 19th chapter and the 19th chapter comes after the great tribulation. Notice the reference following this verse. *"But the beast was captured and with it the false prophet ... The two of them were thrown alive into the fiery lake of burning sulfur." Rev. 19:20*

We know from scripture exactly when the beast is destroyed. We read about it in Revelation 19, at the end of the great tribulation. Jesus comes, gathers us to Himself and fights the beast and his army and destroys him. It is so clear. It all happens after the great tribulation.

The Lord comes in Revelation 19 to make war. The result of the war is that the beast and the false prophet are destroyed and thrown into the lake of fire. 2 Thessalonians 2 says that the Lord will destroy the Antichrist by the splendor of His coming. Given these Biblical truths, how can the second coming of Christ happen before the great tribulation? According to the Bible, it is impossible.

Look again at Revelation 19.

"But the beast was captured, and with it the false prophet who had performed the signs on its behalf ... The two of them were thrown alive into the fiery lake of burning sulfur." Rev. 19:20

The beast is destroyed in Revelation 19, at the very end of the great tribulation. That is when the Lord comes. Jesus destroys the Antichrist by the splendor of His coming. There is no pre-trib-rapture.

Chapter Four

Two in the Field

One Will Be Taken

Two are in the field and the big question is this; when Jesus comes, which one will be taken? People who believe in a rapture say that Christians are taken at the second coming. Time after time, however, the Bible makes it clear that the sinner is taken, not the Christian. The sinner is taken away and put in Hades (Hell). We will look at several verses to prove this point.

"The kingdom of heaven is like a man who sowed good seed in his field. But while everyone was sleeping, his enemy came and sowed weeds among the wheat ... 'Do you want us to go and pull them up?' 'No ... Let them both grow together until the harvest. At that time I will tell the harvesters: <u>First collect the weeds</u> and tie them in bundles to be burned; then gather the wheat.'" Mt. 13:24,25,28,30

Do you see which one is taken first? The scripture says, "<u>First collect the weeds</u>." The weeds are taken, not the wheat. Then starting in verse 36, Jesus explains that the field is the world and the good seed represents the sons of the kingdom. The weeds are the sons of the evil one. The enemy who sows them is the devil. The harvest is the end of the age and the harvesters are the angels.

It is very clear, at the end of the age two are in the field, but it is the sinner that is taken first, not the Christian. This is enough proof to explain that the sinner is taken and not the Christian but let us look further at this subject.

Matthew 24 says:

"Noah entered the ark; and they knew nothing about what would happen until <u>the flood came and took them all away. That is how it will be at the coming of the Son of Man</u>. Two men will be in the field; one will be taken and the other left. Two women will be grinding with a hand mill; one will be taken and the other left. ... You must be ready for the Son of Man will come at an hour when you do not expect him. ... Who then is the faithful

and wise servant ... It will be good for that servant whose master finds him doing so when he returns. ... he will put him in charge of all of his possessions. But suppose that servant is wicked and says to himself, 'My master is staying away a long time,' and he then begins to beat his fellow servants and to eat and drink with drunkards. The master of that servant will come on a day when he does not expect him ... <u>He will cut him to pieces and assign him a place with the hypocrites, where there will be weeping and gnashing of teeth</u>." Mt. 24:38-41, 44-50

From these verses we learn that the second coming will be like the judgment that came in the time of Noah. <u>The sinner was taken away in the judgment not the saints</u>. Noah was delivered from the judgment but he stayed in the ark, on the planet.

We also see that when the master returns, after being gone for a long while, that <u>the sinner is cut to pieces and sent to Hell</u>. Notice also that the wise servant is kept there on earth to care for the master's possessions. The faithful one is not taken away; the sinner is taken when the Lord returns.

Vultures Eat the Sinners

When Jesus returns, a couple of things happen simultaneously. The believers are resurrected from the dead and, along with the Christians who are still alive, they receive new bodies. It happens in just a flash. The Bible says it happens in just a twinkling of an eye. So, instantly fast! Then immediately, they go to earth and Jesus kills the sinners. It is those sinners that are taken but the Christians remain on the planet.

Let us look at the scripture in Matthew 24 that shows us that the sinner is taken. The sinner is killed. His body is eaten by birds and his spirit is taken away to Hades. When scripture says one is taken and the other is left, it is referring to the sinner's spirit being taken away to Hades. All of the sinner's spirits will stay in Hades until judgment day.

"For as the lightning that comes from the east is visible even in the west, so will be the coming of the Son of Man. Wherever there is a carcass there <u>the vultures will gather</u>." Mt. 24:27-28

Notice, how this scripture in Matthew fits together with the verses in Luke 17 below.

""I tell you, on that night two people will be in one bed; one will be taken and the other left. Two women will be grinding grain together; one will be taken and the other left." "Where, Lord?" they asked. He replied, "Where there is a dead body, there <u>the vultures will gather</u>."" Lk. 17:34-37

Jesus talks about vultures eating people. It is not the Christians who will be eaten by vultures when the Lord returns. It is the sinners who Jesus kills who will be eaten by the vultures. Their bodies are eaten and their spirits are taken away to Hades. We read about this again, and in more detail, as we look at the second coming in Revelation 19.

"On his robe and on his thigh he has this name written: King of Kings and Lord of Lords. And I saw an angel standing in the sun, who cried in a loud voice <u>to all the birds</u> flying in midair, "Come, gather together for the great supper of God, so that you may <u>eat the flesh</u> of kings, generals, and mighty men, of horses and their riders, and the flesh of all people, free and slave, small

and great. ... The rest of them were killed with the sword that came out of the mouth of the rider (Jesus) on the horse, and all the <u>birds gorged themselves on their flesh</u>." Rev. 19:16-18, 21

The second coming, as described in Matthew 24 and Luke 17, fits with the end of the great tribulation in Revelation 19. Revelation 19 is at the back of the book. After all the things described in Revelation chapters 1 through 19, then, and only then, does Jesus return. Jesus does not come before the great tribulation.

From these verses we see that Christ's second coming will be like lightning that can be seen from the east to the west. We learn that when Jesus comes He will kill sinners and their bodies will be eaten by vultures. When Jesus is explaining about two being in the bed and one is taken, the disciples ask where it will happen. At first His answer seems strange. Jesus tells them wherever the dead bodies are, there the vultures will be. In other words, it will happen all over the world. Sinners will die and their bodies will be eaten by the birds but what will happen to their spirits? Their spirits go to Hades and they do not live again until one thousand years have passed.

"The rest of the dead did not come to life until the thousand years were ended." Rev. 20:5

Christians Reign With Christ

The Christians remain on the earth to rule and reign with Christ for a thousand years.

"They had not worshipped the beast or his image and had not received his mark on their foreheads or their hands. They came to life and reigned with Christ a thousand years." Rev. 20:4

So, what do we learn from this chapter?

1. One is taken and the other left.

2. It is the sinner that is taken away in the judgment.

3. Vultures eat sinners and their spirits are taken to Hades (Lk. 16:23-26).

4. Christians remain on the earth. They are caught up and in a flash they come down immediately and Jesus puts them in charge of His possessions (Mt. 24:45).

5. There is no pre-trib-rapture because all of this happens at the end of the book of Revelation and not at the beginning.

What Will It Be Like?

Many Christians will be on earth during the great tribulation. What will it be like for them? What will happen to them? Here is a verse that gives us a starting place to answer these questions.

"They (the Christians) overcame him (the Devil) by the blood of the Lamb and by the word of their testimony; and they did not love their lives so much as to shrink from death." Rev. 12:11

Christians are amazing overcomers at this point of the great tribulation. They even overcome the devil. For further study about Christians during the great tribulation, I encourage you to read my books, <u>Unexpected Fire</u> and <u>Poetic Fire</u>.

Chapter Five

No Wrath for Saints

Christians Not Appointed to Wrath

The scriptures make it clear that God did not appoint His children to suffer His wrath. The Bible says,

"For God did not appoint us to suffer wrath but to receive salvation through our Lord Jesus Christ." 1 Thes. 5:9

This scripture was part of a letter that was written to the Church in Thessalonica two thousand years ago. The wrath of God that Paul was referring to was not the great tribulation but the wrath of Hell. Think about it: Paul would not write to protect the Christians in his time, to save them from a great tribulation, that was more than two thousand years away. None of the members of the church in Thessalonica would live for that long. They could not possibly be alive at the end of the age, so he is not referring to the wrath of God that comes during the great tribulation. He is speaking about Hell. Hell is the ultimate wrath of God.

Paul was writing to his friends who needed assurance of God's saving grace. God doesn't appoint His children to suffer wrath but to receive salvation from Hell. The judgment of eternal damnation is totally removed when we properly receive the sacrifice of Christ.

Here is another verse about the wrath of God. It is also in the letter to the church at Thessalonica.

"They tell how you turned to God from idols to serve the living and true God, and to wait for his Son from heaven, whom he raised from the dead - Jesus, who rescues us from the coming wrath." 1 Thes. 1:9-10

Once again, Paul is writing to Christians who lived two thousand years ago. He is not talking about God rescuing them from the wrath of the great tribulation. The great tribulation is not the only time when the wrath of God falls on sinners. Hell fire is by far the worst example of God's wrath and that is the wrath that Paul is referring to in these verses. The wrath of God is mentioned 47 times in the New Testament and almost all of those verses are in reference to Hellfire.

The Bowls of Wrath

The wrath of God is certainly mentioned in the book of Revelation. During the great tribulation, we find extreme judgments which come as part of God's wrath against sinners and demons. These judgments include the seven bowls of God's wrath that are released on the earth during the final days of the great tribulation. This wrath of God is not appointed for, nor does it harm, Christians. At no time; not now, and not in the great tribulation, does God appoint His children to suffer His wrath.

Just because God's wrath is not aimed at, or appointed for His children, does not mean that God takes them away in a rapture. He rescues and protects them but not by removing them. Noah was rescued from the wrath of God in his day but he was not taken from the earth.

Supernatural Protection

There are at least 8 different places in the book of Revelation that tell us God extends a supernatural covering of protection over His children during the great tribulation. His wrath is not appointed for believers. In some of these verses, God makes it clear that Christians are not the ones who are appointed for wrath and in the other verses protection is implied. His wrath is judgment and that is for sinners and for the devil. Look at the verses.

1. "Come out of her my people so that you will not share in her sins, <u>so that you will not receive any of her plagues</u>." Rev. 18:4

Only if you share in the sins of the great tribulation do you receive her plagues. Therefore, people who walk with God and separate themselves from sin will not receive any of the plagues that come upon the earth as part of the wrath of God. The saints have supernatural protection.

2. "The first angel poured out his bowl on the land, and ugly and painful sores broke out <u>on the people who had the mark of the beast and worshipped his image</u>." Rev. 16:2

If the sores come on those who have the mark of the beast, it logically means that the sores do not come on those who do not have the mark of the beast. They are protected from the wrath of God. This is one of the bowls of wrath that is poured out. Believers have supernatural protection from the bowls of wrath.

3. "<u>If anyone worships the beast and his image and receives his mark on the forehead or on the hand, he, too, will drink from the wine of God's fury, which has been poured full strength into the cup of his wrath</u>. He will be tormented with burning sulfur ... And the smoke of their torment rises forever and ever." Rev. 14:9-10

Once again, the book of Revelation tells us that the cup of wrath is appointed for the worshippers of the beast. They receive the cup of God's wrath full strength. Those who refuse to worship the beast or receive his mark do not receive God's wrath. Christians will not worship the beast or receive his mark so the wrath of God is not for them. They have supernatural protection.

4. "There is no rest day or night for those who worship the beast and his image, or for anyone who receives the mark of his name. This calls for the patient endurance on the part of the saints who obey God's commandments and remain faithful to Jesus." Rev. 14:12

Here is another verse that speaks of God's protection for His children. Torment and restlessness, night and day, are promised for those who worship the beast and receive his mark. This is the wrath of God. Therefore, protection from torment and restlessness will come to those who do not worship the beast. Notice also, that the saints are present on earth at this time and they are exhorted to have patience, obey God's commandments, and remain faithful.

5. *"Do not harm the land or the sea or the trees <u>until we put a seal on the foreheads of the servants of our God</u>." Rev. 7:3*

This is a mark of divine protection. The next verse tells us why the servants of God received the seal on their foreheads.

"And out of the smoke locusts (demons) *came down upon the earth and were given power like that of scorpions ... They were told not to harm the grass ... but <u>only those people who did not have the seal of God</u> on their foreheads." Rev. 9:3-4*

The servants of God are given a seal on their foreheads so they will not be tormented by locust demons during the great tribulation. The servants of God do not suffer the wrath of God.

A mark of God's protection was also placed on His children who lived in Egypt in the time of Moses. They put the blood of a lamb on their doorposts and God protected them. The death angel passed over them instead of killing the firstborn of those families. This kind of supernatural protection is shown in several places throughout the Bible.

6. *"Then I looked, and there before me was the Lamb, standing on Mount Zion, and with him 144,000 who had <u>his name and his Father's name written on their foreheads</u>." Rev. 14:1*

Again, we discover a verse that shows the name or seal of God and of the Lamb, on the foreheads of those who stand with Christ. This is a mark of divine protection.

7. *"I looked and there before me was a pale horse! Its rider was named Death, and <u>Hades was following close behind him</u>. They were given power over a fourth of the earth to kill by sword, famine and plague." Rev. 6:8*

Early in the time of the great tribulation, the fourth apocalyptic horse of God's judgment brings plagues. Symbolically, the rider is called Death and symbolically, Hades follows him. Together with the other apocalyptic horses they kill a quarter of the people on the earth. Notice, that Hades (Hell) follows Death. Those who are killed are going to Hades. In the great tribulation, Christians do not go to Hades, which is a type of Hell. It stands to reason therefore that those who are killed are unbelievers and not Christians. Once again we see that the children of God are protected from His wrath and judgment.

8. "When the dragon saw that he had been hurled to the earth, he pursued the woman who had given birth to the male child. The woman was given the two wings of a great eagle so that she might fly to the place prepared for her in the dessert, where she would be taken care of for a time, times and half a time, <u>out of the serpent's reach</u>." Rev. 12:13-14

These verses are not about the wrath of God but about protection of the saints from the attacks of the devil. During parts of the great tribulation, Christians will be persecuted and some will become martyrs for Christ. In these verses, however, we are told that, for a time, God protects His children from the devil's attacks by keeping them out of the serpent's reach.

Rescued from the Coming Wrath

In conclusion, Revelation makes it clear that the wrath of God is appointed for sinners and Satan. Christians who are alive and remain until the coming of the Lord are protected from the wrath of God. They are not appointed to suffer God's judgment or wrath.

We also discover that Christians are present during the great tribulation. For a season, God will protect His people even from persecution, but at other times believers will become martyrs for Christ. They will die because of their faith in the Lord Jesus and because of Satan's attacks. No Christian, however, is tormented or killed because of the wrath of God. There is a reason for everything the Lord does and the death of martyrs always causes sinners to come to Christ. The Lord never allows His children to suffer persecution without giving them the grace to endure. He tells us that the rewards in eternity far outweigh the afflictions we may suffer on earth.

Part Two

Additional No Rapture Verses

Chapter Six

Jesus Stays in Heaven

Collaborative Verses

Any doctrine in the Bible should be well supported by complimentary verses throughout the scriptures. We should be wary of any doctrine that is built on a single verse. Wherever you go in scripture, you will discover the truth that there is no pre-trib-rapture.

The Bible confirms the return of Christ after the great tribulation. The coming of Jesus during the days of the last trumpet, the resurrection of the dead, and the end-time battle all take place at His coming. The marriage supper of the Lamb is our reward after these things are over, therefore, by His grace, we need to endure to the end.

We will look at some portions of scripture that rapture theorists use to bolster their ideas. We will show you, in fact, that these verses are not in support of a pre-trib-rapture but tell us that there is no such thing.

Jesus Stays in Heaven

The Bible tells us that there cannot be a pre-trib-rapture because Jesus must stay in heaven until after the great tribulation. He does not come out of heaven until the end of the book of Revelation.

"Repent, then, and return to God, so that your sins may be wiped out, that times of refreshing may come from the Lord, and that he may send the Christ, who has been appointed for you - even Jesus. <u>He must remain in heaven until the time comes for God to restore everything</u>." Acts 3:19-21

We see in this scripture that Jesus comes only when the restoration of everything begins. At the beginning of the book of Revelation, the world will be in a mess and it will get worse. The great tribulation starts. Instead of evolution we have devolution, where everything is destroyed piece by piece. The destruction comes in ever-increasing measures until the full strength of God's fury and judgment falls.

It takes 7 years for the judgments and destruction to be complete. When the 7 seals are removed from the scroll, war, famine and plagues kill about two billion people (Rev 6:8). When the 6th seal is removed people cry out for the rocks and mountains to fall upon them so they will be taken out of their misery (Rev 6:16). That is not a picture of restoration, so it is not time for Jesus to come out of heaven.

Then the 7 trumpets are blown and brimstone, meteorites and asteroids crash into the planet destroying a 3rd of the life in the sea, burning a 3rd of the vegetation on the earth, and poisoning a 3rd of earth's drinking water (Rev 8). Worse than that, demons like locusts come and torment the sinners for 5 months (Rev 9). That is certainly not the restoration of all things, so Jesus cannot come yet.

During the last half of the great tribulation the beast, the false prophet and the great harlot bring havoc and mayhem to the world. Evil rises to a new level and Christians must go undercover.

Then on top of that, the 7 bowls of God's wrath are poured out on the earth. The Bible says that with these God's judgments are complete. They are absolutely devastating. Revelation 16 describes them: people break out in sores, all life in the sea dies, all surface water becomes poisonous, the ozone layer is depleted (the sun scorches the earth), the worst earthquakes in history decimate the planet, and hailstones weighing up to one hundred pounds each come crashing down from the sky, killing everything in their path. This, by any stretch of the imagination, is not the restoration of all things. By the time the great tribulation is over, the world is just about uninhabitable and the battle of Armageddon begins.

At the end of that battle, the time for restoration begins. Jesus comes in the middle of the battle to restore everything. He overturns the destructive momentum that has covered the earth. Just as the scriptures say, He must remain in heaven until the time comes for God to restore everything. This is one more reason why there is no pre-trib-rapture. Jesus is not leaving heaven and coming to earth at the beginning of the great tribulation. He comes as depicted in Revelation 19, at the end of the book, when restoration is about to begin.

Chapter Seven

Saints Ready for War

Christ and His Armies

There is no pre-trib rapture. We now know that Jesus must remain in heaven until the time comes for God to restore everything. When He does come, however, He brings His sons and daughters with Him from heaven. They are ready for war. The disciples of Christ fight alongside of Him, when He comes.

"See, the Lord is coming <u>with thousands upon thousands of his holy ones</u> to judge everyone, and to convict all the ungodly of all the ungodly acts they have done in the ungodly way, and of all the harsh words ungodly sinners have spoken against him." Jude 14 -15

"They have one purpose and will give their power and authority to the beast. They will make war against the Lamb, but the Lamb will overcome them because he is

Lord of lords and King of kings - and <u>with him will be his called, chosen and faithful followers</u>." Rev. 17:13,14

"I saw heaven standing open and there before me was a white horse, whose rider is called Faithful and True. With justice he judges and makes war ... <u>The armies of heaven were following him dressed in fine linen</u>, white and clean." Rev. 19:11,15

In these verses, we discover that when Jesus returns, He comes to make war, and His faithful followers are with Him.

Resurrection

When believers die today, they go to be with the Lord. Paul said, *"To be absent from the body and to be present with the Lord." 2 Cor. 5:8 KJV*

Our bodies stay on earth and turn to dust but our spirits are immediately with Jesus in heaven. At the second coming, Jesus comes riding a white horse and all of the spirits of believers come as well. When we come, we are riding white horses just like Christ (Rev 19:14). When we get into the clouds our bodies are raised from the earth in the resurrection. At that moment, our bodies join our spirits that are coming down with Jesus. Then we shall be like Jesus for we will see Him as He is. After being changed in a twinkling of an eye, we come down to the earth with Jesus to fight against hardened sinners and demons.

To sum it up, at that time two things happen for believers:

1. At the second coming, believers receive a resurrected, incorruptible body.

2. At the second coming, believers join with the Lord in the great end-time battle to destroy evil and start the restoration of all things.

This teaching of the end-time battle is found throughout the scriptures. Here is one passage from the Old Testament that describes this battle.

"I will gather all nations to Jerusalem to fight against it … <u>Then the Lord will go out and fight against those nations</u> as he fights in the day of battle. On that day his

feet will stand on the Mount of Olives, east of Jerusalem." Zec. 14:2-4

That scripture is in reference to the second coming and it happens during the battle of Armageddon. Jesus comes on a horse. He dismounts and His feet stand on the Mount of Olives in Jerusalem.

This is an Old Testament scripture, so it is not only cherished by Christians but by Jews as well. At the second coming, some Jews do not know that Jesus is Messiah, but they know that when the Messiah comes He will stand on the Mount of Olives in Jerusalem because they read it in Zechariah 14. They also know that His millennium reign begins at that time for further on in the same chapter, we read:

"The Lord will be King over the whole earth. On that day there will be one Lord, and his name the only name." Zec. 14:9

The Jews studied and embraced these verses of scripture long before Christians did. They know that when the Lord comes, the resurrection of the dead will happen as well. That is the reason for a phenomena that I see every year when I travel to Israel. I am referring to the massive Jewish cemetery on the Mount of Olives.

This cemetery has been used for over 3000 years and has over 70,000 graves. There are many who believe that those who are buried on the Mount of Olives will be first to be resurrected on the day of the Lord for that is exactly where He will be standing.

This cemetery site stands as a monument to the ancient teaching that the resurrection, the coming of the Lord, and Messiah standing on the Mount of Olives all happen at the same time.

Jesus stands on the Mount of Olives during the battle of Armageddon just after raising the dead to life. Therefore, Jesus does not come at the start of the great tribulation for that is not the time appointed for the resurrection, the battle of Armageddon, and for Him to stand on the Mount of Olives.

Once again, the Bible reveals that there is no pre-trib-rapture.

Chapter Eight

The Days of the Last Trumpet

Timing the Trumpets

The book of Revelation describes 7 seals, 7 trumpets and 7 bowls of wrath. The bowls of wrath happen in the days of the last trumpet (see Revelation 10:7). It is at the end of that season when Christ comes.

Jesus comes in the days of the last trumpet when the mystery of God is accomplished. He does not come at the blowing of the 1st trumpet and Jesus certainly does not come before the 1st seal is broken, as rapture theorists suggest. Let us look to see what the Bible says about the last trumpet.

"Listen, <u>I tell you a mystery</u>: We will not all sleep, but we will all be changed-in a flash, in the twinkling of an eye, <u>at the last trumpet</u>. For the trumpet will sound, the

dead will be raised imperishable, and we will be changed." 1 Cor. 15:51-52

We receive the following information from this verse.

1. The mystery of God, spoken of through the prophets, is the resurrection of the dead.

2. The resurrection mentioned leads to eternal life and incorruption. From that time the saints will be changed; they will have an imperishable body.

3. The resurrection of the dead takes place at the last trumpet. We are not raised back to life sometime before the 1st trumpet sounds. We are not resurrected before the 7 seals are broken, that initiate the start of the great tribulation.

We discover further details in the book of Revelation.

"<u>But in the days</u> when the seventh angel is about to sound his trumpet, the mystery of God will be accomplished, just as he announced to his servants the prophets." Rev. 10:7

The last trumpet signals the start of the last section of the great tribulation. Notice, it says - <u>'In the days when the seventh angel is about to sound his trumpet.'</u> There is a short period of time that involves some days. These days are connected with the 7th trumpet. They include the days of the pouring out of the bowls of wrath and are finalized by the second coming of Christ and the resurrection of the dead as seen in Revelation 19:11-19.

When the last trumpet is blown the final details are put in motion. We read:

"<u>The seventh angel sounded his trumpet</u>, and there were loud voices in heaven which said: 'The kingdom of the world has become the kingdom of our Lord and of his Christ, and he will reign forever and ever.'" Rev. 11:15

When reading through the verses that talk about the blowing of the 7 trumpets, we discover that as each is blown a catastrophic event occurs on earth. When the 7th trumpet is blown, however, no catastrophic event happens. Instead of catastrophe, a prophecy from heaven is released. It says, "The kingdom of the world has become the kingdom of our Lord."

The 7th trumpet prophecy tells us what will soon unfold. It releases the last details before the second coming of Christ and the resurrection of the dead.

This is concluded with the pouring of the last bowl of wrath during the battle of Armageddon. We read:

"Then they gathered the kings together to the place that in Hebrew is called <u>Armageddon. The seventh angel poured out his bowl into the air</u>, and out of the temple came a loud voice from the throne, saying, <u>'It is done!</u>" Rev. 16:16-17

Following this, in a moment of time, the final judgments come. Immediately, we see the return of the Lord and the resurrection of the saints. It takes all of Revelation chapters 17, 18, and 19 to describe everything that is happening on earth and what is happening simultaneously in heaven. It all happens in just a moment of time. In the days of the sounding of the last trumpet Jesus comes and the mystery of the resurrection occurs.

The timing of the second coming is connected with the last trumpet. Specifically, there are 7 notable trumpets blown at the end of the age. Jesus comes and gathers His children to Himself during the days of the blowing of the seventh trumpet. It is the last one mentioned in the book of Revelation. The last trump is connected with the resurrection of the dead as we read in 1 Corinthians 15:52.

This tells us that there is no pre-trib-rapture. The Bible never speaks of such an event. It does not exist.

The Feast of Trumpets

Some teachers refer to the Feast of Trumpets as further proof of a pre-trib-rapture. There are 7 feasts of the Lord that were instituted for the Jewish people and written about in Leviticus 23. Although, at this time it is mostly the Jews who celebrate them, each feast is actually fulfilled in the life of Jesus Christ. Four of them are celebrated in the spring of the year and three are observed in the fall. It is common for believers to see the spring feasts as being fulfilled during the time of the 1st coming of Christ. The 3 fall feasts line up with the second coming of Christ, and the summer months represent the season of time between the two comings of Christ. Presently, we are still in that period of time between the two comings of Christ.

Because Jesus' second coming starts with the sound of a trumpet and takes place in the fall season, it is easy to think that this Feast of Trumpets lines up with the second coming. It is feast number 5 and happens before the 6th and 7th feasts. It is assumed that it refers to a pre-trib-rapture - a rapture that would supposedly take place before the great tribulation and the millennium reign of Christ, which rapturists say are feasts 6 and 7.

This is a very weak argument. Yes, the last 3 feasts do point to the return of the Lord but not a pre-trib-rapture. The return of the Lord happens at the end of the book of Revelation, during the days of the blowing of the 7th trumpet - the last trump. No trumpet is blown at the beginning of the book of Revelation.

The biblical record detailing the Feast of Trumpets is very short and simple. The people were to blow the trumpet and treat the day like a special Sabbath. They dedicate that day to the Lord and do no work. They consecrate themselves and prepare for judgment day and the resulting glory of God. Punishments would be for sin and rewards for righteous living. All of that happens at the end of the great tribulation.

In the entire Bible, there is only one place where we see the Feast of Trumpets observed. We read about it in Ezra 3:6. After the Israelites return to Jerusalem from their captivity in Babylon, they celebrate with the Feast of Trumpets. During this feast, they began the first stages of dedicating the desecrated temple back to the Lord.

If this is an indicator of its end-time significance, the Feast of Trumpets will commemorate the start of the rededication of the temple in Israel after Babylon no longer controls it.

Remember, that during the great tribulation, the newly built Jewish temple will be desecrated because the image of the beast will be set up there. All people will be forced to worship that image that is set up in the temple but true believers will refuse. At the end of the great tribulation, at the coming of Christ, the beast is thrown into the lake of fire and Jesus will remove that abomination and will set up His throne in the temple.

The Feasts of Trumpets does point to the second coming of Christ. It takes place at the end of the great tribulation; just before the temple, God's people, and the whole earth is rededicated unto Him. The idea that this feast refers to a pre-trib-rapture is completely unfounded. A pre-trib rapture totally contradicts every other bit of evidence on the subject. There is no pre-trib-rapture.

Chapter Nine

Friend of the Bride Groom

John and Jesus are Baptizing

People who speak of a pre-trib-rapture will often refer to the words of John the Baptist when he talks about the friend of the bridegroom. In this chapter we will look at what this scripture says to see if it is in reference to a rapture.

"After this, Jesus and his disciples went out into the Judean countryside, where he spent some time with them, and baptized. Now John was also baptizing at Aenon … [some came] to John and said to him, "Rabbi, that man who was with you on the other side of the Jordan-the one you testified about - well he is baptizing and everyone is going to him." To this John replied, "A man can receive only what is given him from heaven. You yourselves can testify that I said, 'I am not the Christ but am sent ahead of him.' <u>The bride belongs to the bridegroom. The friend who attends the</u>

bridegroom waits and listens for him, and is full of joy when he hears the bridegroom's voice. That joy is mine, and it is now complete. He must become greater; I must become less."" Jn. 3:22-30

We see two different people that John speaks of; the bride and the friend who attends the bridegroom. Some, who believe in a rapture will say that one of these is the church and the other is a special group that are taken away in a pre-trib-rapture. The context and content of these verses do not say that at all, nor do they add any credence to a rapture doctrine.

All Bible students know that the bridegroom is Jesus and the bride is the church who belongs to Jesus. That is confirmed throughout the scriptures, but what about the friend?

The Friend of the Bridegroom

The friend who attends Jesus is John the Baptist.

John, says that the friend who attends the bridegroom waits and listens and is full of joy when he hears his voice. Then he says, as clearly as can be, *"that joy* [of being the friend] *is mine and it is now complete"*.

In other words, John prepared the way for the coming of Jesus the bridegroom. He attended and connected the Church with Jesus. The revelation of who Jesus was, was revealed to John when he baptized Him. As He came out of the water, the Holy Spirit rested on Him like a dove. John then heard God's voice from heaven say to Jesus , *"You are my Son, whom I love; with you I am well pleased."* Lk. 3:22.

John is Jesus' friend. They were cousins and they grew up together. These scriptures do not speak of friends, plural, but of a friend, singular and John makes it clear that he is that friend.

John is full of joy when he hears the voice of Jesus. He knows that Jesus has received everything that He has from heaven. He is attending Him as the bridegroom's friend. Finally, to further clarify the point, John goes on to say that this joy is his <u>and is now complete</u>.

It is problematic to connect these scriptures about John the Baptist with a rapture. John says it is about his personal role and partnership with Jesus. He is excited to play his part and once he baptizes Jesus, preaches, and makes proclamations about Him, his task and his joy are complete.

The scripture speaks of John in this way; *"I will send my messenger ahead of you, who will prepare your way"* - *"a voice of one calling in the desert. 'Prepare the way of the Lord, make straight paths for him.'" And so John came . . ."* Mk. 1:2-4

John is God's chosen attendant for Jesus. He is the friend who attends the bridegroom. These verses have nothing to do with a rapture. They do not point to a rapture or add any credence to a rapture doctrine. These verses are about Jesus, the Church and John the Baptist. There is no pre-trib-rapture here.

Chapter Ten

The Ten Virgins

Ten Virgins

Another portion of scripture that is often used to bolster pre-trib-rapture theology is the parable of the ten virgins. It is found in Matthew 25:1-13. The parable is about 10 virgin women. They have kept themselves pure but 5 are wise and 5 are foolish. They all fell asleep because the bridegroom took a long time to come. The wise ones had extra oil but the foolish ladies did not. Suddenly, the cry came that the bridegroom had arrived. The foolish ladies who had no oil asked the wise to give them some of their oil because their lamps were going out. The wise refused and instructed them to go and buy some. Then the bridegroom came and went into the wedding feast and the door was shut. When the foolish ones finally come to the feast, they called to the Lord to let them in. He then told them that He did not know them. Finally a warning is given to keep watch - to be prepared - for we do not know the day or the hour of the Lord's coming.

Most rapture enthusiasts believe that the wise virgins are those who the Lord will take away to heaven in a pre-trib-rapture. This scripture, however, has nothing to do with a rapture. It is about being ready for the return of the Lord. It is about being welcomed into the marriage supper of the Lamb.

For our discussion, the most important detail of this parable is the timing of when the Lord comes. Does He come before the great tribulation or at the end of the great tribulation? It would be helpful, therefore, to see when the marriage supper of the Lamb takes place. The time of the marriage feast is the time that the story of the 10 virgins takes place.

Revelation Makes it Clear

The book of Revelation brings things into perspective and makes the matter of timing clear.

In several places it instructs us that the story of the 10 virgins takes place at the end of the great tribulation.

1. As we have seen, the Lord comes back in Revelation 19 at the end of the book of Revelation. There is absolutely no mention of His return before that chapter and that is clearly after the great tribulation. We read in Revelation 19:

"I saw heaven standing open and there before me was a white horse, whose rider is called Faithful and True ... his name is the Word of God. The armies of heaven where following him, riding on white horses ... On his robe and on his thigh he has this name written: King of Kings and Lord of Lords." Rev. 19:11,13,14,16

2. Another proof that the ten virgin's story takes place after the great tribulation is the time placement of the marriage supper of the Lamb. It certainly does not happen at the beginning of the great tribulation. It takes place at the end of the book of Revelation in the very same chapter when the second coming of Christ takes place. The

wedding supper begins in the 19 chapter of Revelation. We read:

"Let us rejoice and be glad and give him glory! <u>For the wedding of the Lamb has come, and his bride has made herself ready</u>." Rev. 19:7

Later, in the same chapter we read the response of the angel. Of course, once again we see that this is after the great tribulation, at the end of the book of Revelation. The angel instructs John to write about the wedding supper that has finally come.

"Then the angel said to me, "Write: Blessed are those who are invited to the wedding supper of the Lamb!' And he added, "These are the true words of God."" Rev. 19:9

This verse about the wedding supper of the Lamb, (Revelation 19:9) comes immediately before the second coming of the Lord in verse 11. This could not be more clear.

The Main Thing

For the purposes of our discussion, how we interpret the details of the scripture about the 10 virgins is immaterial. The main point when talking about a rapture has to do with when the Lord is coming; before or after the tribulation. Theologians may have differing views about who the virgins are or what the oil or the extra oil in the flasks represent. They may differ on what they think the shut door means or how the foolish virgins managed to purchase the oil later. All of those details ultimately are important, and I certainly have a perspective for each of those details in the parable myself. Our discussion, however, is about a rapture. The story of the 10 virgins cannot be connected to a pre-trib-rapture for it takes place at the second coming of the Lord and it is about virgins coming to the marriage supper the Lamb. Both of those things happen after the great tribulation and not before it.

A Thief in the Night

We will say more about the 10 virgins but let us gather more details first.

3. There is a 3rd verse in Revelation that points to the fact that Jesus comes at the end of the great tribulation. Notice the warning in Revelation 16, just before the return of the Lord. It is very much in line, with the story and warning given to the 10 virgins. We read:

"<u>Behold, I come like a thief! Blessed is he who stays awake</u> and keeps his clothes with him, so that he may not go naked and be shamefully exposed." Rev. 16:15

Near the end of the great tribulation, just before the Lord's return, Jesus warns that He will come like a thief in the night when people find it hard to stay awake. So we must be vigilant; we must be ready. This is a similar theme to that of the 10 virgins.

We are warned to stay awake, and to have our clothes ready. People who believe in a rapture talk about Jesus coming as <u>a thief in the night</u>, and so He will. Even a rapture-focused movie was made about this. It was called "<u>A Thief In the Night</u>". Perhaps those who made the movie overlooked the timing of this warning. These believers might not know that the warning continues near the end of the great tribulation. It is found here in Revelation 16, not at the beginning of the book. Jesus does not come as a thief in the night before the great tribulation. He comes as a thief in the night at the end of it, just like scripture says.

Jesus Taught About the Marriage

Let us read what Jesus taught on the subject of the marriage supper of the Lamb. It is recorded in Matthew.

"The kingdom of heaven is like a king who prepared a wedding banquet for his son. He sent his servants to those who had been invited to the banquet to tell them to come, but they refused to come. ... Then he said to his servants ... "Go to the street corners and invite to the banquet anyone you find." So the servants went out

into the streets and <u>gathered all the people they could find, both good and bad</u>, and the wedding hall was filled with guests. But when the king came in to see the guests, he noticed a man there who was not wearing wedding clothes. ... Then the king told his attendants, "<u>Tie him hand a foot, and throw him outside, into the darkness, where there will be weeping and gnashing of teeth</u>."" Mt. 22:2,3,8,9-11,13

Jesus taught about the wedding supper of the Lamb. The wedding supper is the thousand-year reign of Christ on the earth. The great tribulation is the time of the harvest of the earth. The greatest revivals in history take place during the time of the great tribulation (See Revelation 7:9 and 14:14). Notice, in Jesus' teaching, that God instructs His servants to gather both good and bad people for the wedding supper. The wedding supper of the Lamb is not just for a few elite, special people. In the end, His banquet hall is full.

That is called the harvest of the earth. Jesus taught, *"The harvest is the end of the age."* Mt. 13:39

Notice also, that someone got into the millennium (the wedding supper) but he was not wearing the right clothes. Because of it, he was cast out and thrown into Hell. We read in Revelation 16, verse 15 that Jesus warned His people to make sure they were wearing the right clothes. They are the clothes of Christ's righteousness that His faithful followers wear. These clothes are only worn when people put their trust in Jesus and what He did for them on the cross, and they have righteous acts that follow their faith.

At the end of the millennium, Satan is released to tempt the nations and many follow him and are judged and thrown into Hell. For more details on those who are mortal during the millennial reign of Christ, read my book <u>Unexpected Fire</u>.

Back to the Ten Virgins

With this understanding of the millennium, we can return to the story of the 10 virgins and answer the question about the foolish virgins. It is in keeping with the teaching of scripture that the foolish virgins are those who are not ready for Christ's return at the end of the great tribulation. Later, they come and ask the Lord to let them in to the wedding feast. In the parable, He does not say no to them, but only that He does not know them.

There are those who do not know the Lord at His appearing. They do not receive glorified bodies but are allowed to enter the millennium for other reasons (see my book <u>Unexpected Fire</u>). It is as though they are given another chance. The Bible speaks of this in Isaiah 11:11 and Zechariah 14:16.

There are both mortals and immortals in the millennium. Those who become immortal are the believers who are made like Christ at His coming. We also know there are mortals there because, at the end of the millennium, when Satan is released to deceive the nations, many of them march with the devil against Jerusalem and they are killed. They can only be killed if they are mortal (Rev. 20:8-9).

Some of those foolish virgins will acquire the robes of righteousness and some of them will not

(Rev. 19:7-8). That is why Jesus casts the man, not wearing the wedding garments, from the wedding supper and into Hell (Mt 22:13).

The great white throne judgment and Hell fire happen after the millennium is over. Those who sided with the devil will be judged and cast into Hell (Rev. 20:11).

The coming of Christ, the wedding supper of the Lamb, and the story of the 10 virgins happen after the great tribulation. Once again, we discover there is no pre-trib-rapture.

Chapter Eleven

Coming Back in the Same Way

The Ascension

As we near the close of our study, we will look at the ascension and return of Christ. The days between the resurrection of Jesus and His ascension into heaven were extraordinary for the disciples who were present. Surprisingly, there is no record of Jesus performing any healing miracles during these forty glorious days before He was taken up into heaven. Instead, at that time, Jesus focused on teaching about the Kingdom of God.

During those days, He taught His disciples about His kingdom coming to earth. His teaching about the kingdom involved the people of Israel because the teaching led His disciples to ask when He was going to restore the kingdom of Israel. Jesus told them that it was not for them to know the times or dates that the Father has set for the kingdom of Israel to be restored. He knew that the restoration of the kingdom of Israel was in the distant future. I am sure He did not want them to be distracted from their present mandate.

The disciples' mission would move forward when the day of Pentecost had fully come. Jesus told them that they would receive the out-pouring of the Holy Spirit and then they would be anointed for powerful ministry. This ministry would enable them to lead people to salvation, minister to them with supernatural authority, and introduce them to the purposes of Christ's kingdom.

What is the teaching of the kingdom? Jesus' teaching about the kingdom of God gave the disciples a global perspective of God's rule and reign on the earth. From that time forward the teaching of the disciples changed. After Pentecost they spoke of the restoration of all things that would come, that God commanded every person to repent, that Jesus is both Lord and Christ, that every knee shall bow and every tongue shall confess that Jesus Christ is Lord, and that God accepts from every nation the ones who fear God and do what is right. The gospel went to the nations.

The kingdom of God was no longer just about Israel, but about the rule of Christ over every nation. It is about His government coming to earth and the need for every human being to bow before Jesus and His kingdom reign. The completion of this mandate is what the second coming of Christ is all about.

Jesus is Taken Up

Immediately, after Jesus had spoken about the kingdom of God and the promised gift of the Holy Spirit, He was taken up into the clouds before their very eyes. This took place on the Mount of Olives in Jerusalem, overlooking the temple mount.

"After he had said this, he was taken up before their very eyes, and a cloud hid him from their sight. They were looking intently up into the sky as he was going,

when suddenly two men dressed in white stood beside them. "Men of Galilee," they said, "why do you stand here looking into the sky? This same Jesus, who has been taken from you into heaven, <u>will come back in the same way you have seen him go</u> into heaven."" Acts 1:9-11

After Jesus left, two angels spoke to the disciples. They gave them words of comfort and left them with an amazing expectation of the second coming of Jesus Christ. Since that day, disciples have been anticipating, that one day, the skies over Jerusalem will open and the Messiah will return. The angels said that Jesus will return in the same way the disciples saw him go. Here are some similarities between Christ's ascension and His return:

The Same Way

The angels said, *"Jesus ... will come back in the same way you have seen him go."* Acts 1:11

1. Jesus rose upward, supernaturally at His going. He will descend downward, supernaturally at His coming.

2. He vanished into the clouds when He left, and He will emerge from the clouds when He comes back.

3. He left from the city of Jerusalem when He was taken up and He will return to Jerusalem when He returns.

4. He was seen by a multitude who gazed on him intently at His going. Every eye will see Him at the time of His coming.

5. He was accompanied by disciples and angels as He left. He will be accompanied by disciples and angels when He returns.

6. His feet were standing on the Mount of Olives when the time came for Jesus to leave. His feet will, once again, stand on the Mount of Olives when He comes back.

7. He was the King of kings and Lord of lords, the eternal Son of God, when He rose. When He

returns He will still be the King of kings and Lord of lords, the eternal Son of God.

No Return to Heaven

At the second coming of Christ, Jesus instantly emerges from the clouds with His newly resurrected family. He descends and stands on the Mount of Olives. Then, Jesus fights as in the day of battle. He finishes the battle of Armageddon and He takes over the world. His coming back to Jerusalem, in the same way He left, confirms once again that there is no pre-trib-rapture because that battle happens at the end.

There is no mention anywhere, in the whole Bible of Jesus returning to Heaven with His bride. There are so many scripture verses, on the other hand, that speak of Jesus immediately setting up His kingdom on the earth, when He returns at His second coming. It will be a kingdom of righteousness.

Then it will be said, *"The kingdom of the world has become the kingdom of our Lord and of His Messiah, and he will reign forever and ever." Rev. 11:15*

"I will gather all nations to Jerusalem to fight against it … <u>Then the Lord will go out and fight against those nations</u> as he fights in the day of battle. On that day his feet will stand on the Mount of Olives, east of Jerusalem… The Lord will be King over the whole earth. On that day there will be one Lord, and his name the only name." Zec. 14:2-4, 9

Jesus Rules From Jerusalem

The Bible gives us great details of how Jesus will rule, and where He will rule from, when He comes back to the earth.

"In the last days <u>the mountain of the Lord's temple</u> will be established as chief among the mountains; it will be raised above the hills, and all nations will stream to it. Many peoples will come and say, "Come, let us go up to the mountain of the Lord, to the house of the God of Jacob. He will teach us his ways, so that we may walk

in his paths." The law will go out from Zion, the word of the Lord from Jerusalem. <u>He will judge between the nations and will settle disputes for many peoples</u>. They will beat their swords into plowshares and their spears into pruning hooks. Nation will not take up sword against nation, nor will they train for war anymore. Come, O house of Jacob, let us walk in the light of the Lord." Isa. 2:2-5

After Jesus returns the whole world will want to go up to Jerusalem, to the mountain of the Lord's temple. This is the temple mount. The nations will stream to it because they will want to be near Jesus. They will thirst for His teachings and He will settle disputes and bring peace to the whole world. This scripture is not about heaven. It tells us what will happen on the earth after Jesus returns.

This will be so great! All who love His appearing cry, "Come quickly, Lord Jesus."

Chapter Twelve

Rapture Teaching is Dangerous

Rapture Distractions

Some people may now be convinced that there is no pre-trib-rapture. They may think, however, "What is all the fuss about? Does it even matter?" The answer is a resounding "Yes!"

The teachings about a pre-trib-rapture may be one of the most dangerous, popular teachings in the evangelical Church today. I do not want to dwell on this but it will help us to focus properly if we take account of this present rapture mindset. Not everyone who embraces a rapture doctrine is guilty of everything on the following list, but certainly, everyone who embraces a rapture ideology is guilty of some of these dynamics, at some level.

Negative aspects of a pre-trib-rapture theology

1. A huge amount of pastoral teaching is <u>focused on a pre-trib-rapture</u> in the evangelical church. Some congregations make this the main subject of Sunday morning sermons. That means that, by default, many things that should be taught are not being taught in the Church.

2. The <u>rapture doctrine is non-biblical</u>. False teaching and all false doctrine will lead people astray. It is a misrepresentation of God's word and His ways. This book has proven that the rapture teaching is not found in the scriptures. Those who emphasize and teach such doctrines will, one day, lose their credibility. This will cause young, immature believers to become discouraged when they see that their leaders and their focus has been so far off. Then, they will not know who they can trust and what they should believe. Some will feel as though they have been duped. Some may even lose their faith because of it.

3. Many <u>Christians have embraced a terrible fear</u> of the great tribulation and the last days because

of a rapture theology. Even though it is a false teaching, a rapture has become their only hope. In Matthew 24, Jesus tells us not to be afraid of the judgments of the last days, but Christians are still afraid. Rapture teaching has not emphasized the protection of God's people and their amazing partnership with Him in the great tribulation. Fear of the future is a serious problem in the evangelical Church.

4. Some <u>believers have an escapist mentality</u> because of the rapture teachings. This is so dangerous because some are not focused on the mandates of God's word but only on getting off of the earth. They only think about getting out of here. A large number of disciples are not interested in developing a New Testament Church model. The development of the five-fold ministries, the care of sinners, addressing the political climate in their nation (Eze. 22:30, Jer. 29:7), and occupying until He comes (Lk. 19:13 KJV) are completely ignored by many because of a rapture expectation. Some are not interested in being a godly influence in this world by taking the

high ground of government or being a change-maker in society. By default, they have given this place over to the devil.

5. Some Christians have <u>no concept or desire for revival</u> because they just want a rapture. The harvest of the earth is the end-time purpose of God's people. The greatest revivals of all time are still ahead of us, but a huge number of Christians are completely disconnected from this. The Farmer of Heaven looks patiently for the harvest of the earth. Many believers are completely out of step with the heart of God and His big picture because they have been distracted by so much rapture teaching. They have missed the heart of God.

6. Some believers have <u>no focus on or love for Israel.</u> They have no concern or prayer for what God is doing with His chosen people because they are impassioned with a rapture theology. They are not seeing Israel as God's prophetic time clock. They have no focus on the Jews or the Holy Land and that usually means they are not blessing Israel, in any way. When Christians do not bless and support Israel, at this time in the plans of God,

they rob themselves of the fullness of God's promised blessings. Whoever blesses Israel and God's purposes with Israel, will be blessed (Gen 12:3). Some Christians are really missing this.

7. Equipping the saints for the work of the ministry is the main role of the five-fold ministers of Christ that we read about in Ephesians 4:11. We need teaching, training, and equipping but if our teaching is off we will not train or equip. Many Christians are enjoying worship, fellowship and Bible study but very few are being equipped to do the work of the ministry. Most <u>leaders do not know how to equip the saints</u>, and many <u>saints do not want to be equipped</u> for this purpose. They have not focused on this directive. The teachings of a rapture have shifted their focus away from equipping. We are in need of a dynamic paradigm shift that will line us up with the goals and behavior of New Testament Church life.

Time to Prepare

If the great tribulation were to break forth today, much of the church would be totally unprepared. Most would not understand what is happening or what their role in the last days might be. It is time for a new focus and for preparation to get underway.

Our theology determines our worldview and that will determine our attitudes. Our attitudes will determine our choices and behavior. So, a theology shift is where things must begin. Once our teaching lines up with God's word, then we will become serious about how our behavior must change. Then, ministers will learn to train and equip the saints for ministry. Jesus is the author and the finisher of our faith. He will shift His Church into preparation mode, in His time. Get ready for it.

Share The Truth

After reading this book, many of you will begin to understand the seriousness of this subject. Some will be excited to learn the truth and will begin to prepare with earnest. Others, however, may be discouraged and feel a sense of panic, because they know that so many people have embraced a rapture theology. They know that many in the church have been climbing a ladder but the ladder is leaning against the wrong wall.

Some may experience worry or fear when they realize that they may have to face the traumas of the great tribulation. To them, I say, "Do not be afraid. God's wrath will not be released on His people and many will be protected from persecution. God will not allow you to suffer beyond the availability of His grace. This will be the most amazing time in history to be alive. The miracles, signs and wonders and the supernatural provisions will be the greatest ever seen. To top it off, the revivals will be absolutely exciting. If the Lord takes you, you will be with Him. If you remain until His appearing, you will welcome Him with shouts of Hallelujah and glory.

Be Kind

Finally, let me encourage you. Fix your eyes on Jesus. Don't attack others who have a rapture theology. It will take time for some to change their view on this matter. Share the message of this book as positively as you can with as many people as you can. Look for God's timing and be led by the Holy Spirit when you share this, because rapture theology is deeply imbedded in the minds of mainstream evangelicals.

Do not reject or distance yourselves from those Christians who believe in a rapture. They are your brothers and sisters and must be honored and respected.

Pray and ask the Lord to help you share this message and pray for the opening of eyes and understanding for those who have a different perspective.

Be a partner with Heaven in the end-time purposes of God. It starts with the right theology. May God help you as you press forward. May you be excited with this mission. May you hear the words of your Heavenly Father, "Well done, my good and faithful servant." Pass it on.

Further Study and Information

For further study on the book of Revelation and the end-times go to PeterWyns.com. You will find the following material and much more created and produced by Dr. Peter Wyns. It will be both informative and practical. Some of the books include - Unexpected Fire, Poetic Fire, Israel's Coming Revival, and America in the Last Days. A number of audio and video materials are also available on this theme. For all other inquires reach us through the contact information listed in the first pages of this book.

www.ingramcontent.com/pod-product-compliance
Lightning Source LLC
Chambersburg PA
CBHW050441010526
44118CB00013B/1632